Live Your WHY!

Ryan Stm

PBL Stories and Structures:
Wins, Fail, and Where to Start

PBL Structure and Stories: Wins, Fails, and Where to Start

Ryan Steuer

PBL Stories and Structures:
Wins, Fails, and Where to Start
© 2018 Ryan Steuer

This book is available at special discounts when purchased in quantity for use as premiums, promotions, fundraising, and educational use. For inquires contact: ryan.steuer@magnifylearningin.org

Published by Magnify Learning Inc.
Indianapolis, IN
www.magnifylearningin.org

DEDICATION

This book is dedicated to all who live their 'why'
every day in the service of others.

.

CONTENTS

CONTENTS

PBL Stories and Structures:
Win, Fails and Where to Start

INTRODUCTION
Live Your Why

S kyler was disengaged in school for years. His only real view of the future was to figure out how he can find more time to skate with his friends. School was alright in Skyler's eyes because it was a decent meal, and he could hang out with his friends. The annoying classes didn't get in the way too much if you were quiet. As Skyler floated along, he ran into a group of teachers doing Project Based Learning that would disrupt his status quo of continually underachieving. Skyler is the student that you have right now, who has the ability to perform well, but no desire or motivation. You know the kid who can find the error on your test but doesn't take the time to try on the same test. Or the one who messes up your whole thinking around grading because she doesn't do any of the homework and still aces the test. You just thought of a couple of names, didn't you? That is one of the great things about being an educator! All of our stories have names and faces and destinies!

Let's continue Skyler's story and move from his past to his destiny. The generational poverty Skyler grew up in gave him a lot of negative momentum showing him that school did not matter.

Like most teenagers at the time of the publishing of this book, he has an Instagram account. He started taking pictures at the bus stop and posting them. After a while, he noticed he was getting a small following, so he decided to get a more advanced camera. He added pictures of his buddies and nature from state parks. Then one day Time magazine asked if they could feature a few of his photographs and things started to change for Skyler. Skyler began getting 5,000 followers a day until he reached 48,000!

Time magazine features one Instagram account in each state in the country. Depending on where you live, your representative is likely a photojournalist or a freelance photographer. If you look up Time Magazine Instagram 50, you'll see Skyler as the Indiana representative for a couple of years in a row at the age of 17! Quite a ways to climb from a kid whose most substantial previous ambition was to skate and hang out. Skyler now has a website where you can buy his photography and sponsors like Coleman, Valvoline and other brand names you recognize. He used education to find a path to his dreams.

I can't claim to have ever helped Skyler hold a camera, but he will tell you the year he first experienced Project Based Learning was a significant shift for him. He learned the importance of learning and community. Becoming a lifelong learner has served him well, as he now has become a self-taught freelance photographer and Instagram influencer. If we only would have focused on compound sentences instead of helping to create problem solvers who can apply critical thinking, we would have done Skyler and many other learners a disservice. Project Based Learning can be the structure and culture building vehicle to help you engage your standards as you inspire learners the way you have always wanted to. You have a Skyler in your classroom waiting to be involved and pointed toward his dreams.

Project Based Learning changes lives because it empowers a person to reach their highest potential under their own fruition and opens opportunities otherwise thought impossible. In short, PBL allows teachers to be in their sweet spot. The real reason you accepted your calling as an educator. Nobody enters education because they want kids to be average or to master a standardized test. We launch into education because we want to help young people achieve new heights. We see they don't understand their full capability, and we want to open their eyes to their true options.

PBL is a different type of instructional model. It's hands-on and active, but it is also minds-on and has times of reflection, contemplation, and problem-solving. This book is written the same way. Stay active as you read by having a current project idea or project nearby, so that you can create and revise as we collaborate but note that much of this process will be you working through your own instructional practices and mindset. My hope is you will be open to finding the best way to reach your students. To help you visualize what this may look like in your classroom, every chapter will have an explanation of a major PBL pillar, a fail story, a win story, the bottom line, and a note on how to get started. The chapters follow the PBL process but can also stand-alone, so feel free to skip to a section that meets your immediate needs or scoot through them to see the big picture.

At this point, we assume you have figured out the current educational model based on the Industrial Revolution needs to shift. Passive learning and compliance will only lead to excellent point gatherers, which as of the writing of this book does not lead to a future we want for our learners.

At the beginning of the project based learning movement, we started with a fantastically engaging entry event that ended with students performing excellent presentations, and in the middle, we had this thing called "the mess in the middle." The change in instructional practice was and is necessary, but the earlier work has been refined. The raw pioneering work matured, and we have a structure and process that can be followed methodically to make sure all learners are on a path to success. Innovation will always be in education with massive room for personalization, but there need to be structures we operate from that will enhance our creativity.

While the need for lifelong learners has always been around, the future is going to call for problem-solving engaged learners who can communicate their passion. Schools will likely still be hubs of content, but with content at our fingertips, information is not the answer. We have all of the answers we need. The winners of the game of life are those who can use data to achieve goals and apply it to help others. Marketing gurus say this book should start out amplifying the problem, but you are entrenched in the issues of school, so let's get started on the solution!

For years now, I've started every professional development session with Simon Sinek's TedTalk on the golden circle because it points us to our 'why'. The golden circle contends effective communication starts from the why, how, and then the what. In our daily conversation, we often start with the what and don't even get to the why which empowers us. For instance, 'What do you do?' is a typical introduction question. You can use the usual process and say "I am a teacher", which then allows the other person to project their idea of a teacher on you. What if you answered with your why first? "Because I believe kids have immense potential waiting to help the world, I inspire today's youth to be lifelong learners who look at the world as a set of problems they can help solve.

I do all of this through my calling as a teacher." Try it next time you hear the question. Your conversation will be much more fruitful. Guaranteed!

So why project based learning and why now? For me, project based learning became a necessity after I realized one of my students had dropped out of high school the first semester of his freshman year! I left the world of Industrial Engineering so that I could save the world as an 8th grade English teacher, and it didn't seem to be working for everyone. I had stories of learners doing great things too, but I came into teaching to help all kids see more opportunities. I was working hard for kids, building relationships, and doing the best I knew how, but it didn't take too long for me to realize that passion and love weren't enough.

As a former engineer the logic was simple, if what I was doing wasn't working, I should change. A colleague was dabbling in Project Based Learning, so I jumped in. We made mistakes, and we let the students know we made mistakes, and we all learned together. The results were there at the end of the day though—attendance went up, discipline went down, standardized test score rose, and my students became learners who could solve their own problems. I was fulfilling my 'why'. Most of our 'why's are the same. We all want our students to have the best opportunities available, which may mean a 2-year or 4-year college, trade school, or straight to the workforce. Mostly, we want our students to be happy with their choices and be equipped to do well in their chosen endeavors. For me, PBL has been the vehicle to get students to this place.

<u>Chapter 1</u>

It's Working, and It's Spreading

Inevitably when you hear about project based learning, someone will say, "I have been doing PBL for years. We just didn't name it." I propose the PBL in this book is different than the traditional projects you did in class. Authenticity and community partners will be a big part of the difference, but there is also a structural difference to the flow of learning, which is key to the success of your efforts. Many of the same resources you have passionately been using for years will still apply to PBL; we just need to change the order to build inquiry and empowerment. Typically, a project launches after the learning has taken place, but in PBL, we want to launch the project idea and problem right at the beginning. Let me give you a real-world example, and then we will launch into the process. You'll feel the difference.

You may be a bit uncomfortable, which is good because that is where most learning takes place.

We all have great projects where we get out in the community, and kids get their hands dirty, and things happen, but see if you can feel where this project based learning unit changes the dynamic of the classroom to empower students. When working with Mrs. Wisdom's third-grade class, we started with an entry event to launch and address two of her most difficult subjects from her experience: perimeter and persuasive writing.

All of the third-grade classes gather in one room for the Entry Event, and instead of starting out telling this young group about standards in kid-friendly language, we inspired them with a worthy problem to solve. We brought in the executive director of the local senior center. Many of the learners have never had access to a person who is in charge of a social service organization, so the meeting alone broadens horizons. The executive director talked about how senior citizens are not getting proper nutrition when they stay home, and the lunch at the center is where they get the bulk of their healthy diet. Would these young philanthropists like to help out? Cheers ensued as the third graders realized they were going to be helping others. The next portion of the Entry Event involved me asking the third graders if they would want to help the center by building raised garden beds. More cheers. I then asked if anyone knew how we could figure out how far around a garden bed it would be so that we could buy cinder blocks. After some mumbles, I finally heard someone sheepishly say, "perimeter?" in a tone only used in classrooms. "Yes!" I exclaimed. "Perimeter! Who here knows how to use perimeter so well they can help us build raised garden beds?" Now, I spent my time in an 8th-grade classroom, so I didn't know that every time a guest asks a question in a 3rd grade classroom every hand in the room goes up. So, I rephrased, "How many of you will not miss any answers on a quiz about perimeter?" Most of the hands went down, and I said, "Friends, this is not good. Do you want to help the senior citizens at the center?" Cheers. I continue, "How will we help them out if we don't know perimeter?" Dramatic pause. "Is there anyone in the room who could teach us perimeter?" Dramatic pause number two. "Mrs. Wisdom, could you teach us perimeter?" "Yes, in fact, I have been teaching perimeter for ten years now," she returns. "Young world changers, how many of you want to have Mrs. Wisdom teach you perimeter so that we can help the senior citizens at the center?" Cheers. Maybe you get the same reaction when you launch your perimeter unit. There is the shift! By starting with the why of perimeter, we have a room full of learners excited to engage perimeter.

Mrs. Wisdom then goes on to teach much of the same perimeter unit she had in previous years. Best practices still need to take over as she utilizes data well to personalize the learning through workshops, but the why runs through the entire unit and continues to drive the project. PBL is not replacing all of the years of education study you have done, but it is going to reorder things and give you a structure.

<u>Chapter 2</u>
Step 1 - Identify the Problem

The key to finishing a project well is starting a project well. To help you feel the flow of a PBL Project, we will walk through the next six chapters in the order of steps within a project. Before launching a project, we identify the standards and the real-world problem our learners will be solving. We will launch our project with an Entry Event meant to build enthusiasm for the project and to layout the desired outcomes.

In planning a project, we start with the standards we are going to engage in this project. Partly, because we live in a world engrossed in standardized testing, but also because this is the basis of the content we want our learners to engage. If we are addressing a real-world problem, we are going to run into standards left and right. In the real world, people are reading and writing non-fiction texts, creating budgets, figuring perimeter, performing experiments, and so on. Find the meaty standards with the most upside, whatever it is you call them – power standards, critical standards, etc. Basically, choose argumentative writing over Haikus.

Once you have a set of standards you are going to engage, you can launch your Entry Event to Identify the Problem. To ensure the authenticity of your problem, plan to have a community partner come in to launch the Entry Event. If your problem is a real-world problem, there should be real people in the real world working on this real problem. These people will want to come in and talk to your learners because people want to help and are passionate about their work. We will cover community partners in depth in Chapter 8. For now, you need a real-world problem your learners can participate in through your standards. To frame the problem throughout the project, develop a driving question.

Your driving question will be the umbrella under which all aspects of your project will take place, so it needs to be open-ended, have multiple solutions, and at the very least be non-Googleable. The driving question will be a home base for your PBL. When you are in the heart of genetics in Step 3 talking about Pundit Squares, you can reference back to your driving question to remind learners of the why, "How can we help educate families about genetic diseases when their children are first diagnosed?" This noble why will guide the deep content learning and bring about empowerment and engagement as learners are no longer learning content just to pass a test.

At Risk Driving Questions	Proficient Driving Questions
Why do we need slope intercept formula?	How can we help people understand the relationship between supply and demand?
What are the causes of the Civil War?	How does a divided country negatively or positively affect the future success of a nation?
What causes genetic diseases?	How can we help families whose children have genetic diseases?
Let's learn perimeter!	As landscape architects, how can we help build raised garden beds for the local Senior Center?

To develop a benchmark for Step 1, have your learners develop a Problem Statement. A problem statement has learners restate the driving question to display they understand their role and assignment. To complement our genetics driving question, a problem statement may state, "As a genetics specialist, I will create a public service announcement to educate parents about the genetic disease of their child." The generic format follows, "As a (role), I will (action verb with end product) so that (what happens because of the work). Learners should be able to show a well thought out problem statement before moving on to Step 2. Embedded in the process is creating an opportunity for our learners to see themselves in roles that may be new to them. Learners are now writing how they are an author, marketer, scientist, educator, museum curator, or whatever role you have for them. Role identity has a significant impact on how learners see themselves in the future.

Your Entry Event will build excitement, inquiry, and engagement around your project. Doesn't that sound like a great way to start a unit? Step 2 will communicate your expectations to learners.

Fail Story

I decided to take on world hunger with my learners. I presented the real-world problem to them and waited for the magic to happen. It turns out all my learners thought all hungry people were in Africa and that the primary solution to this problem would be canned goods. I wanted to protect their voice, so I ran with it. I asked them how they would afford the shipping costs, and they wanted to have a car wash. I asked them how they would provide the materials for a car wash, so they tried to sell suckers. And on…and on…it grew!

Eventually, I stopped the madness and suggested we try to help out the local food pantry. At which point, one student mentioned his mom volunteered there and could take anything we wanted to the community center for free. Sanity triumphed, and we made a difference in our part of the world with the influence we had at the time.

Win Story

The director of the Benjamin Harrison Home came in to launch an Entry Event. He had a real-world problem. The Benjamin Harrison Home went out to schools to perform workshops. The elementary school workshops were well utilized, but the middle school courses were rarely requested. The director charged our students with the task of creating the next generation of programming for the Benjamin Harrison Home. In the Entry Event, learners experienced the original middle school programming with the idea that our learners would be the ones creating a new program for schools across the state to purchase. What a real-world problem to solve! 8th-grade learners were going to write programming for a real non-profit organization for real-life schools to buy and run with students. There were some stipulations, which is a nice lead in to Step 2. The budget was $500, the presentation could not use WiFi, and needed to address content standards for middle schoolers. The goal was to engage the content of the Benjamin Harrison Home and make it exciting for middle school learners. The authentic audience was the Benjamin Harrison Home, which would select the best programming to implement. A powerful why making a difference beyond the walls of the classroom.

Bottom Line: Authentic Project Based Learning should have its foundations in standards and a real-world problem.

Where to Start

Start by digging into your standards and developing your power standards. Not all standards are created equal. For instance, haikus are a standard just like argumentative writing is a standard. One of these two is more likely to help your students problem solve, back up their answers with reason, and perform well on standardized tests. Hopefully, you know which one, but either way you should engage in the conversation. Developing power standards is not a new idea. The discussion has already started, so do some research and see what others are doing. Twitter or Google are pretty good places to engage in this conversation.

Once you find some power standards, you have an excellent place to start a project. Immerse your project in authenticity and standards. It is hard to discover an authentic problem that doesn't relate to standards. Knowing which standards are going to best empower your learners for the future is a reliable place to start whether you are ready to jump into PBL or not.

Chapter 3
Step 2 - Success Criteria

With Step 1 complete, you have launched an authentic, standards-based problem, and your learners are excited to engage in a solution. Step 2 is the process of adding structure to the problem to ensure you lead learners down a successful path. The popular mantra has been, "We need to make space for kids to fail." There is some truth in the statement as our learners need a place they can be empowered to do the work, but it's even more exciting to see our learners succeed after they struggle! It's our job to set up the environment for the best chance of success. On the practical side of this chapter, we are going to bring up rubrics and limits related to the project, which will drive our Need to Knows. In Step 1, learners are dreaming of solutions to a problem. They may be dreaming of camel rides, hot air balloons, and satellites dropping food for those in need. Dreaming is a crucial component to success, but our learners have likely never really engaged in real-world problems and don't understand the liability, permits, and cost of bringing their ideas to fruition. Our job in Step 2 is to add appropriate structure and encouragement to ensure success. Structure does not kill creativity.

While research backs up the benefits of structure, the allegory of the school for the blind illustrates this idea well. Facilitators at an elementary school for blind learners were trying to help maximize recess. The learners had 2 acres of playground to play on, but each day the learners would step out the door and go about 20 yards away from the door. The learners could hear the cars on the other side of the two-acre playground and would stay close to the door despite the consistent assurance of their trusted facilitators that they had plenty of room to go out and play. A new facilitator joined the staff who understood the importance of structure as a safety net to bring more creativity, and she suggested a fence on the outskirts of the playground. With the fence installed along the road at the far edge of the playground, the learners cautiously walked out toward the new fence. With the guidance and encouragement of their facilitators, the learners went out and touched the fence and heard the cars. They ran and cartwheeled back toward the school with some occasional somersaults. From that day forward, the learners knew where the fence was. They knew the fence was there and the space in between was for them. They can now explore the playground on their own and know the structures will keep them on the right track. Structure is good for our learners and us.

One important piece of structure is a rubric. Rubrics should be presented to learners early in a project, so they know what the expectations are. We are going to present rubrics early so that we can generate inquiry. As learners look through the rubric, they will encounter ideas they have not learned about and will have questions. These questions will come out as Need to Knows and will help drive sustained inquiry throughout your project. For instance, when a learner encounters the word angioplasty on your rubric, they are going to need that defined to achieve their project goal. We let them ask the question, "What is angioplasty?" and we say, "Great question! Thank you for asking that. We are going to need to have mastery of these terms to solve this problem. I'll schedule a workshop to help answer your question." What you have just done is validate their question, provide confidence you will answer future questions, and open the door for you to teach a workshop on one of your standards. Need to Knows will continue to build:

- "When is this due?"
- "Do we get to work in groups?"
- "What technology can we use to present?"
- "What is a compound-complex sentence?"

Need to Knows vary in importance, so it is helpful to organize them into categories for yourself and learners. Find categories that work for you, but you need to separate a logistical Need to Know such as "When do we present?" from the content-driven Need to Know "What is angioplasty?" The Need to Knows document should be a living document, to help sustain inquiry throughout the project. As the project begins, you will start to answer Need to Knows through workshops, and together we will move ideas over to a Know column. The constant movement from the Need to Know category to the Know category will show everyone learning is taking place and learning is on-going. As learners develop more knowledge of a topic, more focused Need to Knows will arise, which is another great experience. Validating the new Need to Knows will begin to build a culture of inquiry.

What do I do if my core standards do not come up within my beginning Need to Know session? There is an art to Need to Knows. We want our learners to be empowered to drive their learning, but we also want to lead them to new heights they would not achieve on their own. Questions such as:

- "Did anybody notice in the middle of the rubric where it talks about Pundit Squares? Do we know what Pundit Squares are?"
- "How many of you have ever written a letter to a local government official? Would a workshop on writing a letter be helpful?"
- "I know you have studied western cultures before, but would anyone like a refresher workshop?"
- "Did you notice we are using at least two new technologies? Does anyone want a workshop about the different possibilities we have?"

Any of these questions is more empowering than a list of things we must do because the state says we have to. Once you have a Need to Know on the board, you have license to teach it out, so make sure your core standards are on the list. If you haven't perfected this art form yet, you may need to say, "Hey everyone, this didn't come up, but I need to hold a workshop on XYZ. I think it will help you do ABC, so I'm going to put it up here. Is that ok?" In the context of Need to Knows, adding workshops this way is still better than you have to learn this because I said so.

Data-driven Need to Knows is another way to make sure you are holding workshops your learners need even if they do not ask. If you ask a room full of 8th graders if they know compound sentences, the majority of them will say, "Of course! We did those in 6th grade!" What they are really saying is a bit different, and it's not because they are being difficult or misleading. Every learner has their own unique take on everything we say. To some they are saying, "Of course!" because they remember sitting in 6th grade talking about compound sentences, some could recognize them, others may even use them correctly sometimes, and others still have them mastered. A well-crafted twenty question pre-test on sentence type can create defined groups with different instructional needs. These data-driven Need to Knows cannot be argued because the data can show whether a learner has this Need to Know or not.

Ultimately, the Need to Knows you establish give you significant leverage for the inevitable education question, "Why are we doing this?" With a solid Need to Know process, you can truthfully answer, "We are running this workshop because you asked me to. Remember, this workshop is based on this Need to Know and will help enhance your project idea." Again, a much better answer than our typical answers of "Because the state says we should" or "Because you will need it in college."

Did you feel the switch? Learners are now asking you to teach! In one or two days, you have launched an engaging project and set up a structure to help guide your learners to a successful outcome. You have framed your standards in the real world with a 'why' that is larger than a grade. Now the learners are pushing instead of you pulling them along. Once the problem is identified and structured, we are ready to start looking at possible solutions.

Fail Story

In one Need to Know session, I stopped to answer a Need to Know because I thought it would add clarity. Good intention, but instead what happened is I ended up skewing all of the other Need to Knows. I stopped to talk about one of the new technologies we would be using in the project, and suddenly we ended up with a whole list of technological Need to Knows, which were not part of the power standards I was trying to lead learners to. To fix the problem, I took the Need to Knows from my other class periods and melded them together to create a more complete list that still authentically came from my students. It takes practice, discipline, and trust to give the learners some control over their learning. If we want to have learners actively participate in their education, we have to give them a voice.

Win Story

Developing success criteria with learners can be a big win because we make sure learners are headed in the right direction. When I move rubrics up to the front of the work I am assigning, I find learners are much more likely to be on the right track. All of my students turned in the first three projects I assigned as a PBL teacher. This completion rate was monumental considering I was used to the typical 20% or so learners who just wouldn't bother. This success actually led to more grading on my part because everyone turned things in, but a good problem to have. I attribute much of the success here to the clarity learners had from day one of the project. Right out of the gate, learners knew the expectations, and if they had questions, they had ample opportunity and encouragement to ask.

Bottom Line: Success Criteria will show learners where the goal is and the parameters we have to work within.

Where to start

Ask your learners what they already know about a topic and what they need to know to become more advanced in a subject. Give a quick pretest to see what learners already know about your unit. Then take the next step to ask where they are curious. Asking learners questions about what they want to learn is empowering. They will likely guide you in the direction you have already planned, but they still want to have the voice to say they wanted to go that way. Take 15 minutes and try it out.

Chapter 4

Step 3 – Researching Possible Solutions

"Why does the kid who didn't do any work get the same grade as my child?"

"I'll just do all the work because then I know it will be right."

"Well, they just did the work, so I let them."

These familiar statements make all people dread group work. Let's leverage Step 3 as a means to diffuse these often valid comments by keeping learners working individually until Step 4.

Step 3 is a time where we are benchmarking learning immersed in the full context of the project. We are making sure our learners are mastering their standards through content workshops. Now workshops are being created based on learner Need to Knows and the data-driven Need to Knows we created in Step 2. Notice you should be taking grades in these workshops to prove learning. Do not wait to grade all of the content knowledge until the five-minute presentation at the very end. First of all, you cannot grade all of the content standards of four group members presenting during a five-minute period. Secondly, and most importantly, when you try this, the presentation becomes less authentic and more school-ish. Record evidence of learning throughout the process and then let the presentation in Step 5 be as authentic as possible for your professional audience.

For example, you can still have your traditional benchmarks such as quizzes and tests to see if learners have mastered their standards or if they need additional helps. In fact, you want to work on mastering the standards before the presentation for two reasons. First, you want your learners to be extremely prepared to show off their new-found knowledge and expertise. Secondly, after the project is over, it tends to be more difficult to fill in any learning gaps. If we tackle the learning gaps during Step 3, they are still under the umbrella of the project. We also have the added engagement to say, "We are holding this workshop to get you all caught up on XYZ standard, so you are best prepared for your group work and your final presentation." As we help learners catch up, it is useful to have additional context and motivation.

We are capitalizing on the inquiry and engagement we created in the Entry Event. Learners understand the big picture of the project, and they also understand there are things they need to learn to achieve their goal. Now that we have engagement, we capitalize on it with academic rigor!

Fail Story

As I sit ready to show off the great work my learners have created to a panel of community partners, I smile. The project was authentic, it launched well, the end product is exciting, so I wait in eager anticipation. Then I hear presentation after presentation where the most energetic academic learner talks 90% of the time, and the others sit back, watch, and only answer questions directly sent their way. My smile fades, and I ponder. Then I ask questions:

Me: "Why didn't you talk during the presentation?"

Learner: "She knew more than me, so I just let her go."

Me: "You did research though, why didn't you talk about that?"

Learner: "My role was to find pictures off of Google."

Me: "Oh."

Win Story

Based on the Fail Story above, I came away with two critical wins I think everyone should consider. The first is to make Steps 1-3 as individual as possible. The individualization to start creates an environment where everyone is accountable for their own learning. It doesn't mean learners cannot collaborate; it does mean learners cannot hide in a group. Individual quizzes and benchmarks allow us to know who is on track or not before the big presentation day.

The second win of this awful fail story is to ensure without fail that there is a practice presentation day. We MUST have a practice presentation day, so we know what learners are going to say. Presentation day is game day. There is not a whole lot of instruction you can do during a presentation, so you should have a pretty good idea of what the presentations are going to be like before you get community partners in the room. More on the logistics of this in Step 5.

Bottom Line: By the end of Step 3, learners should be equipped to contribute to the group with researched solutions and content knowledge.

Where to start

Create an engaging opportunity for learners to engage in their research. Keep all of your typical benchmarks, so you know things are going in the right direction, but instead of just presenting the information in a lecture, determine which topics need to come from you and which your learners can find on their own.

Scaffold this process if your learners are not used to this by giving them credible websites or apps to go to for the information. Letting untrained learners free to roam Google in hopes that they find useful information is an excellent way to catalog your own fail story.

<u>Chapter 5</u>
Step 4 – Pick a Solution

Now that all of your learners have researched solutions for the problem and participated in content-based workshops, they are appropriately equipped to actively participate in a group. By holding off groups until Step 4, we have created a situation where the bulk of a learner's grade is based on their individual work. We have also created a situation where group members do not depend on each other until they are better equipped and have wrestled with the problems, research, and solutions before entering a group. While keeping things individual until now can help the process, it does not mean that learners know how to efficiently work in teams, divide work, or pick the best solution.

Before we enter into the world of group structures and dynamics, let's put it out there that it is ok to have groups of 1 for an entire project. The first PBL project you embark on may be a great place to try out groups of one. Groups of one will allow you to acclimate to the learning flow of PBL and allow your learners to get used to the new learning flow. Once you are both accustomed to the new vocabulary and structure, groups are a fantastic way to equip our learners with the collaboration skills the workforce is looking for and the general inter-personal skills that are often lacking.

To make sure your first foray into PBL group work has success, it is essential to have enough structure to learn from the failures you will encounter.

Group Contracts

Group contracts are a significant structural and accountability piece, and they add an air of professionalism to the process for learners. Critical components of the group contract are defined roles, strengths/weaknesses, contact information, firing clause, and signature lines. A defined role rewards learners when their area goes well, and we can find out how to bring the group back when things go awry. By listing strengths and weaknesses of each group member, every learner has the opportunity to self-assess and defend why they believe they should have a specific role or not. Listing contact information can do amazing things for problem-solving work through absences and the sharing of data.

A firing clause is not the immediate out that most learners want it to be. In the business world, it is challenging to fire someone for not doing their job well, and the same should be true in your groups. If a learner is brought to the teacher's attention for firing, there should be a teacher-led mediation, redefining of roles, and action items with due dates to ensure that the individual in question has every opportunity to redeem themselves. The firing process can be a learning experience for everyone, but very few learners should get the ax!

Finally, every contract should have a place for learners to apply their signature. Ample emphasis should be placed here to talk up how signing a contract is a promise. When we sign a contract, our character is on the line, and we agree to the terms listed. You may need to do a quick workshop on how to write your signature, which is has real-world value in itself. The signature lines will be a good vehicle to talk about living up to a standard of high character. You will be surprised how many of learners appreciate and live up to this standard.

Group Meetings

Beginning and ending meetings can be another excellent accountability tool. Effective group meetings are organized, short, and specific. The goal of a group meeting at the beginning of a work time is to establish what each member of the group will be working on. The expectations should be very clear from what will be produced to the time it will take to create the work. The goal of a group meeting at the end of a work time is to summarize complete work and establish next steps. End of class group meetings will let everyone see how they are contributing, where they need to focus their energy next, and it gives the teacher a view of where each group is.

How do you make sure that everyone has work to do? Roles defined in the contract can be crucial in answering this question. Some possible positions include leader, technology guru, organizer, researcher, recorder, teacher liaison, etc. You can come up with an endless list, but the real key is in how you define the role. In a recent school visit, I saw a class assign their roles and the definition of those roles. The most popular role was leader because they thought the leader sat around and told people what to do. The facilitator obviously needed to step in and help define the role to clear up this misconception. Another common default role has the lower academic learner spending his/her time on Google looking for pictures. The 'Google pic person' is another role in need of defining to ensure every learner has a challenging role. Defining the roles will help to ensure everyone has a suitable workload.

Another successful tactic is to hold workshops for each person of the group and then have them report back. For instance, have all of the technology gurus report to a 15-minute workshop. At the conclusion of the workshop, have the concrete next steps for the technology gurus to report back to their group. Assigning specific workshops for each position will let you move the workloads around to each person in the group.

To train learners on picking the best solution to the problem they are addressing, the teacher will need to scaffold the process. A decision matrix is a great way to help the process. The purpose of a decision matrix is to value every learner's voice and then to have their idea evaluated on the criteria most important to the project goal. The decision matrix will give the group quantifiable numbers to help them pick a single solution to move forward with. Now the numbers do have a particular amount bias to them since they are being assigned by learners with different viewpoints, but each learner has to commit to a number and then be able to talk to why they selected that number. The result is often the most organized and logical conversation the learners have ever had.

Of all of the steps in the process, this is the most foreign to learners, so every portion of Step 4 should be modeled for learners. A fishbowl protocol is a great way to introduce new concepts such as a group meeting. The teacher and a few other learners model for the class the appropriate way to run a group meeting. The teacher and the group are 'in the fishbowl,' and the rest of the class is watching specific members of the group. The group acts as if they are the only ones in the room and work through their meetings. In the end, the whole class can debrief the strengths and weaknesses of the group meeting shown. This fishbowl protocol will allow learners to see what a successful implementation of these structures looks like and will give the teacher a means of bringing learners back to a shared experience, "Remember in the fishbowl when we established laptops should be closed in a group meeting..."

Groups may seem like a lot work at this point, but they also have a lot of upside for our learners. The ability to work in a group is listed as a key component of success by every workforce leader. Whether our learners are headed straight to the workforce or a post-secondary opportunity, working in a group is going to be a skill they need in their tool bag. To provide opportunities for our learners, we must help them understand how to work in a group. Adding structure and process to groups will help turn the past mess of groups into a future of collaborative success.

Fail Story

Fail stories in groups are not hard to find, and you likely have your own. Here are a few common group fails we are trying to avoid.

- Strong academic learner does all the work
- Group members do the job individually and then just mash it together without any real collaboration
- Group members just talk

- Introverted members do not interact
- Accountability for grades gets tricky

Win Story

Dante: "Our contract says we can fire people, so we want to fire Jason."

Me: "Your contract does say you can fire people. Your contract also states you must have evidence for firing, and your group has to go through a mediation process with me."

Dante: "He doesn't do anything, so we want to fire him. Will you go tell him he is fired?"

Me: "Probably not, but why don't you tell your group to come over here so we can talk about some of the issues you all are having."

The above dialogue doesn't sound like much of a win but having been through many group mediations and only firing one learner, I can tell you these mediations are where most of the productive learning around how to act in a group comes from. Let me give you some dialogue from a group mediation session:

(All three learners look upset, so I am overly cheery)

Me: "Thanks for coming over. I hear you may be

having a bit of a misunderstanding within your group."

All three learners: "Well, he…" and "She said…" and "We want to fire.."

Me: "Let's do this a bit differently. I'd like to run a quick protocol. Let's give everyone some uninterrupted time to tell us about what they see and feel as well as some possible solutions. Dante, you brought this to my attention, so why don't you and Alise start. You have one minute. The rest of us are just going to listen."

Dante: "Well, like I said before Jason isn't doing any work, so we want to fire him."

Me: "Is there anything else you want to say? You still have 45 seconds. Alise, do you want to add anything?"

Dante/Alise: "Nope."

Me: "Jason, how about you?"

Jason: "I don't know what I am supposed to do. They just did a bunch of work without talking to me and then told me to "start doing some work." I would do some work, but they

just keep getting an attitude, so then I didn't
want to do anything."

Me: "Thanks, Jason. Do you have any ideas for a
solution?

Jason: "Nope."

Me: "Well, I see a couple of possible solutions. Dante
and Alise, do you have some specific tasks
you would like Jason to help
with?"

Alise: "Yeah, I guess he could research the effects of
hemophilia on younger kids so that we could
put it in our PSA."

Me: "Jason, do you think you could do that? If yes,
when do you think you could have that done
by?"

Jason: "I could probably get that done by the end of
the period, or I can have it ready by tomorrow
morning."

Me: "Dante and Alise, does that work on your end?

Dante/Alise: "Sure."

Me: "Alright! Let's all check in quickly at the
beginning of the period tomorrow to make

sure everything is copasetic." (Sometimes using big words at the end of mediation confuses teenagers and lightens the mood) ☺

Critical components of a group mediation:

- Use a protocol. Several rounds of individuals are talking or responding without interruption, which lets everyone's voice be heard.
- Make the next steps clear and with a due date.
- Check in to make sure the next steps are completed.
- Have a separate one-on-one check-in if necessary to make sure everyone is alright.
- Spending the 5-7 minutes in group mediation is well worth it.

Bottom Line: Step 4 should establish groups and a single solution for the group to work toward in Step 5.

Bottom Line 2: Groups are hard for adults, so it will take intentional work to make sure groups are thriving. It is worth it!

Where to Start

Group contracts and a decision matrix will give groups structure. Structure is key to group success. Lunch rooms often lack structure or purpose and thus while the learners are in groups very little good comes from the interactions. Start with a group contract you find from someone else and then customize it to meet your specific needs. Look for a group contract that gives everyone in the group a role. A role ensures everyone has a job to do and makes the accountability to that role much more concrete.

Chapter 6

Step 5 – Test, Revise, Revamp, Retest, Present

S tep 5 is a weighty step. You have worked through establishing and teaching useful grouping. Groups will still need to be mediated throughout step 5, but you have modeled successful groups and set up contracts for each group. Success is imminent! It is time to put those groups to work.

In step five, learners will test the solution to the problem that was laid out in the entry event. Hopefully and most likely the solution will fail! TedTalks and blogs tell us failing is a great tool, but what does that mean exactly? The answer from any one learner is likely not going to completely solve the problem so that learners will be using different parts of each group member's ideas. Essentially, everyone's

41

idea failed in some form right off the bat, and that is good! It is a great time to talk about perseverance and revising work to make a better product.

Once groups have a reasonable solution to the presented problem, it is time to test it. An idea should be tested several times before it reaches a final presentation! A tuning protocol is a great way to test out an idea in a very low-risk environment that is mainly about feedback and not about evaluation.

Tuning Protocol Example

Partner A: Present idea to share (2 minutes)
Partners B & C: Clarifying Questions (1 minute)
Partners B & C: "I like…" (2 minutes)
Partners B & C: "I wonder…" (2 minutes)
Partners A: Reflection on the feedback (1 minute)

The above tuning protocol is meant to be modified to fit different contexts, but it proves to be very effective for adults and learners. The above format gives a lot of feedback to the presenting partners, and the other partners get to hear other quality ideas as they give feedback. Here are a few key points as you try out a tuning protocol:

- Time constraints are helpful for creativity.
- Times can be adjusted to depending on the purpose and available times.

- Shorter time frames might be helpful for those new to tuning protocols.
- Clarifying questions are typically short answers or yes/no.
- While learners will eventually be able to run tuning protocols by themselves, a facilitator should be the time keeper to start out.
- As the facilitator of the tuning protocol, I have run this with very large groups.
- The wording of likes and wonders is important

Feedback – You can't do it alone!

A short but important note should be made about feedback here as tuning protocols are introduced. Ron Berger from Expeditionary Learning has two great videos on feedback. The first you can find by googling "Austin's Butterfly," which will show kids the power of peer feedback that is "kind, helpful, and specific." Timely is another excellent adjective to add. The second Ron Berger feedback video you should watch is more of a reflection session of teachers talking about feedback. I have shown it to learners and teachers. It does an excellent job of explaining the power of feedback and the necessity of empowering your learners to give good feedback. Berger uses the example of a class of thirty with one teacher. For a teacher to give two minutes of feedback to each learner would take an entire class period, but if learners could be taught to continuously give kind, helpful, and specific feedback to their peers, then the teacher can be freed up to facilitate the class. This scenario is very possible with protocols and modeling. The tuning protocol gives learners the vocabulary they need to provide constructive feedback politely. By investing the time in teaching the powerful skill of providing meaningful feedback early, a teacher can reap the benefits throughout the year.

The group should do another ongoing reflective assessment through the use of the rubric they received in step two. A possible group role or a rotating role someone takes on could very well be the rubric guru. The rubric guru goes through the rubric to make sure the group is on the right track. Rubric updates should be addressed at the 'beginning of class meeting' to make sure the tasks the group is working on are relevant to the work they need to complete.

The final check before a final presentation is the practice presentation. Practice presentations serve a variety of critical purposes:

- Shows learners where they are missing key components.
- Gives everyone a practice stress event.
- Allows the teacher to hear and see what learners will be presenting.
- Add another benchmark beyond the final presentation.

There are likely additional benefits to practice presentations. The critical logistical consideration for practice presentations is to provide enough revision days between a practice presentation and the final presentation. To find out a presentation has deficiencies and not allow time to fix them is a futile practice.

Practice presentations show learners what they need to work on. A hook that involves a play that the group planned on 'winging' doesn't look so great when performed, or a budget that has to go on a projection screen probably needs another revision to make sure the numbers match up. Youth and adults alike can have a significant plan in their head as they think about the great things they will say to the crowd, but it is a different animal when we have to present it. A practice presentation with the audience looking at different portions of the rubric will help to draw out the key components that are either shining or missing.

Stress can be a good thing! When a class seems to be missing the immediacy of a project, you may want to bump up practice presentations even earlier. Practice presentations can be a great way to show groups that they have a lot of work to do. Again, even without being apathetic about the situation, humans can feel that they are prepared well even though they have an enormous amount of work to do. Practice presentations can serve as an excellent temperature check for groups.

I love having learners present to authentic audiences of community members. It raises the bar for learners and gives them a chance to shine in front of professionals who don't know the great things that are happening in your classroom. However, it is imperative that you know what your learners are going to say! Are they prepared? Are their facts way off? Does everyone get to talk? Did they go off on a tangent and present something weird? The list of questions that you could ask about some of your students could go on and on. You probably just thought of one particular student, didn't you?

Presentation Day

Presentation day is an exciting day, and it should be marketed as such! Yes marketed! You need to sell the awesomeness of presentations to your learners. You say things like:

- "Isn't it awesome that a real bank CEO is going to get to hear your idea?"
- "Can you believe you get to present your architecture plan to a real architect?"
- "I can't wait for you all to share your hard work with our panel of community partners!"

Now you have excited learners! What happens next? Let's talk about the learner side first. The mini-

bottom line here is to make sure your learners are prepared, which admittedly is a massive task. Learners need to be ready with sufficient content mastery and have presentation skills. Step 3 should have shown you where your learners are in regard to content mastery. Let's focus on presentation skills.

Your learners will not intrinsically know what an excellent presentation looks like or how they should act. We need to set up some scaffolding opportunities for them to learn the process we likely take for granted. For instance, one of my favorite workshops of all time is the handshake workshop. We take for granted that learners know how to give a good firm handshake when meeting someone. A quick fifteen-minute workshop can outline the difference between the long creepy handshake, dead fish, and a firm professional handshake. It makes a huge long-lasting difference as our learners look to move toward the opportunities in the professional world. To continue with the professionalism workshop, it helps to talk through the idea of dressing up for a presentation as well. It makes a big difference in how learners see themselves and community partners will always make a note.

Another way we like to communicate in a school setting is via a rubric. Having a presentation rubric is a great way to communicate your expectations to your learners. A quick google search will show you much of this work has already been done, but it is also a good exercise to watch excellent presentations and have learners come up with key attributes for effective presentations. Two important notes on rubrics are to make sure learners receive the rubric at the beginning of the project so they can ask Need to Knows and to make sure you don't grade anything you haven't taught. A presentation rubric will help your learners ask questions about presenting they would not have thought to ask.

A few logistical scaffolding pieces are a presentation schedule, sample questions community partners might ask, and a feedback sheet for community partners. A key to freeing your learners from the fear associated with presenting is to shed as much light on the process as you can. A presentation schedule should be posted for all learners to see as soon as you can, but at least a few days before presentation day. When learners know when they will be presenting, they can start to prepare themselves for their presentations. They know how much extra time they have or do not have.

Community partners are going to be an asset in ramping up the authenticity and importance level of your presentations. At the same time, we do not want our learners 'freaking out' because they have a stranger in their presentation. Providing learners with some sample questions community partners may ask is a helpful scaffolding piece and can be as simple as an exit ticket leading up to presentation day. Have learners answer some of the sample questions below as an exit slip.

- "Why did you pick this project idea?"
- "What was the most challenging part of the project?"
- "What is your favorite part of the project?"
- "If I am going to remember one thing from your presentation, what should it be?"
- "Who else should hear the information in this presentation?"
- "If you could redo one portion of your project, what would you revise?"

You might take this same list of sample questions and include them on your community feedback sheet. It is important for your community partners to give feedback. The feedback makes the community partners feel like they are helping, and your learners will take their feedback very seriously. A simple feedback form of "I like..." and "I wonder..." is a useful tool. It is open-ended enough for any community partner to give feedback no matter their background, and it is simple enough your community partner will not feel overwhelmed. One fear a community partner can have is feeling that they may not be helpful. Handing a community partner a full content specific rubric can backfire because your community partner will be overwhelmed and won't get to enjoy the presentations. Let them enjoy their time with your learners and let your learner enjoy sharing their work. Make presentation day a celebration of the work, not a speech they dread.

Fail Story

Before I was doing practice presentations, I had a student we'll call Rudy. Rudy was from a pretty rough family situation and was behind academically, but he did work for me and tried most of the time. We were sharing poetry in the old-fashioned presentation format to our peers. It was primarily original poetry, so I had given many talks about being kind to others and being great listeners. Rudy was up, and I gave him an affirming look and asked him to come forward. Rudy stepped up to the podium with notes in hand, and we put on our best listening ears. The problem was that Rudy opened his mouth and no sound came out. I calmly affirmed him and told him to take a step back and then start as soon as he was ready. Two attempts and still no words. Not even a stutter! Unfortunately, a young lady in the front squeezed out the smallest giggle. Not a mean cackle but an unintentional giggle. Rudy responded by flipping the entire class the bird with both hands and then walked out. We all sat stunned. As I reflected and as I write, I am slammed in the face by the awful situation I put Rudy in. I put him a fight or flight situation. Would a practice presentation have helped? I think so because Rudy could have practiced the stressful situation, and I would have known what he was planning.

Win Story

This win story is really a turnaround story that shows the power of the process of empowering learners. During a presentation with the largest children's museum in the world in the audience, Sam used a racial slur. Yep. Remember, you can't really teach them up by the time they are presenting. All you can do is listen...and sometimes try to hide.

To make this a win story we need to hear the full growth mindset side of the story. The next year Sam looked at his presentations differently. Sam was engaged in the PBL process and appreciated the culture. His presentation win came during a presentation involving the Civil War. In full costume, Sam presented well thought out ideas to a professional audience. Sam shook people's hands before and after the presentation with a new-found confidence. Sam has the opportunity to define a new life for himself that is much different than the one he has experienced thus far.

Bottom Line: Make the work public. Make the work exciting!

Where to Start

Instead of having your learners present to their peers and you, invite in a community partner. If the community partner is relevant to the topic you are studying, it is a bonus, but if you can't find a geneticist, find any professional who can remark on the presentations of your learners. Bringing in someone from outside of school, ramps up the intensity of your presentations. It is often acceptable and sometimes even 'cool' to give an awful presentation to your peers and teacher. Apathetic presentations are much harder to pull off when the audience has a banker, an architect, and a local small business owner.

Chapter 7
Step 6 - Reflection

Yes! Reflecting on the learning should be happening throughout the project by asking learners for feedback about the effectiveness of workshops, processes, groupings, community partners, and every step you take. By asking learners to reflect, we are showing respect for their voice, improving our work, and differentiating the classroom. Reflection and celebration on the whole project is a good way to bring closure to our project before beginning another.

Let's interrupt this step for a minute and talk about some practical reflection methods that work well in Project Based Learning. Exit tickets that ask learners for "I like" and "I wonder" can reveal a lot about how your project is going and can take as little as 3 minutes at the end of a class period or workshop.

A Chalk Talk protocol from the National School Reform Faculty website can be an efficient way to get quick, meaningful feedback. In a Chalk Talk, learners are all looking and commenting on a specific phrase or question posed by the facilitator either on a chalkboard, dry erase board or piece of chart paper. Then the learners silently write down their thoughts. Learners can comment on the thoughts of other learners. A conversation takes place on the paper instead of with words. Can you think of some wins in this process for some of your learners? Do you have any introverted learners? Any learners that may need to practice thinking before they answer? With a little practice, learners love the protocol as a way to see what others are thinking and as a way to have their ideas publicly displayed.

If you want to share successes and build momentum, a protocol like Bright and Shining Moments usually do it. Bright and Shining Moments asks learners to focus on the great things they experienced during a project. Everything from a community partner interaction to rocking their presentation. Give learners dry erase markers and let them reflect on the best portions of the project by writing thoughts on the board (not by talking). Allow them '+1' an idea if they agree, and watch the different positives start to build up.

If you want to get a more balanced view Roses and Thorns can give you a view of how things are going. Learners share out on a post-it note, or

Chalk Talk the warm feedback (roses) or the cool feedback (thorns). If you use post-it notes have the learners begin to group their ideas and see where patterns emerge. The methods abound, and a quick internet search will load you up with a plethora of ideas, so begin collecting your favorites!

While reflection happens throughout the project, there is still value in devoting a day to reflect and celebrate. Presentation day is a celebration and sharing of the deliverable with a community partner. Reflection day can be a time to reflect and celebrate the class. As you start out, many learners will have never been a part of such an authentic and meaningful project, so it is important to point out to learners the challenging work they have undertaken. As community partners have given feedback and testimonials of their experience, share those with the learners while the work is still up front in their minds. A community partner may have mentioned how she was impressed with their deep knowledge of the subject or how professionally a group presented. Public praise is always a big self-esteem booster, so this may be a time to highlight a few learners who may not always shine in an academic setting. Recognition from a community partner goes a long way, so it is essential to give the community partner an opportunity to provide that praise. When the authentic audience is watching presentations, they can have a feedback form that is "I like" and "I wonder" or maybe even a specific testimonials sheet that the community partner knows will go back to the group.

While the praise and acknowledgment of hard work are essential, we also want to use this time to improve and demonstrate our growth mindset. Groups may need this opportunity to enhance their project if they still need to implement in the community. Ask learners what workshops they may still need based on the feedback from the community partners or to help them prepare for the next presentation. As you are looking for improvements, it is vital for us to put ourselves out there as well, and ask the learners what we can do to improve for the next project (and what we did well). There is a risk as we put our project out there, but this is the perfect time to show that we are also working with a growth mindset. A protocol and careful planning are helpful here to make sure that the session is productive and goes well. Asking the class of thirty teenagers how the project went 'whole group' is not going to get you your desired feedback. Here are some questions to consider as you create a time of reflection:

- How can you make sure everyone's voice is heard?
- How do you make sure overly negative or positive voices don't take over the time?
- How will you respond to the feedback?

- How can you help scaffold the process for learners that have never given feedback to a facilitator?

The last thing you want is a negative free-for-all led by a few strong voices. The second to last thing you want is to be defensive as the feedback comes out. It is appropriate to ask clarifying questions about the learner feedback, and you may have some factors that are forcing your hand such as a district timeline or mandate. You still want to be professional, calm, and open to the learner feedback. Once you have received feedback from your learners, you want to act on it as soon as you can. Even if it is a relatively small aspect, when you act on the feedback learners have given, you are building trust and respect because you have heard their voice. Learners are not accustomed to adults listening to their voice. Learner voice begins to build empowerment and is a major tool in moving learners out of the spoon-fed zone and into a zone of empowerment, pride, and self-motivation.

As you develop a toolkit for reflection throughout the project and as a final step, you will be modeling a growth mindset for your learners. Be open with this process to share with learners the immediate changes that you have made and the changes throughout the years based on learner reflections. You might say, "Based on your reflections from the last project, we are going to take less time during Need to Knows in the next project." Connecting the dots for learners is an essential step in making sure they understand how much you value their opinion.

Fail Story

While group share outs are likely the easiest and most commonly used method of reflection, it can be difficult to make sure you are hearing everyone's voice. At the end of a day, we were moving Need to Knows over to the Know side because we had performed a series of workshops. While I tried to use a "Thumbs up/Thumbs down" to figure out if we should move a topic over, I could tell I was not getting everyone to enthusiastically give me reflective feedback. I pushed on trying to ramp up my energy level and moved many of the topics over the Know side. I was too facilitator focused and thought because I held a workshop on a topic that the learners had mastered the content. Workshops do not always equal mastery! We need to be data driven to make sure we have mastery. If the data shows we need to hold another workshop, let's do that to serve our learners well.

Win Story

We often talk about how failure is a positive, so here is how I was able to turn a fail story into a win story. The next day, based on a tip from a learner, I used a more differentiated and concrete process to determine individual understanding. I would ask the same question about a given Need to Know, but this time, I asked each learner to place a hand over their heart with a number from one to five. One meant that they needed another workshop and five said they had mastered the content. Holding a number in front of their chest gave them an anonymous way to ask for help. The second round did not move as many of the Need to Knows over as I was hoping, but it gave me a much better assessment of the needs of my learners. We ran additional workshops for those that needed them to save the day, but I almost missed a significant portion of learning because I chose a reflection activity that did not meet the needs of my situation.

Bottom Line: Reflection helps solidify the learning and prepare everyone for the next project. Reflection should capture everyone's voice.

Where to Start

Ask learners what they thought about the last you unit you just finished up. You will need to help them a bit because they will not have language for this if it is new. Don't just do this whole group either because you will likely only get crickets, so find a protocol. A chalk talk about Gold and Shining Moments and another for Improvements would work well, or just ask learners to write down two things they liked about the last unit and two things they would change. The key to the whole process is to find one common thread to change and then change right away. Then be public with your actions by saying, "Based on your feedback, you liked having a community partner in the presentations, so we are going to do that again. You also said you didn't like the way you were assigned a topic to research, so for this unit we are going to give you a list of topics to choose from."

Even if you get this wrong, learners will acknowledge that you are trying to listen to their voice. Attempting to listen to their voice permits them to provide you with more feedback on things they like or would like to see modified. It is empowering and part of the process of building a student-centered classroom.

<u>Chapter 8</u>
Community Partners

Community partners are a vital piece of authentic project based learning. Community partners can be involved in any part of the project. Entry Events and authentic audiences are typically good for starting points. As you become more proficient in leveraging relationships with community partners, they can become content experts. Bring in an architect to teach AutoCAD or bring in a DNA specialist to talk about chromosomes.

Community partners are not money! Community partners are much more important than money. The presence of a community partner shows that the work your learners are creating is worth showing up for. Let's talk about how to start and maintain relationships with the community partners.

Relationships with many partners are the key to having them come back again and again and again. If you invite her in and you ask her for money, you're abusing your relationship. If you ask him to come for eight hours on their first visit you are probably harming that relationship. It is your job to bridge the gap and find a natural entry point for your community partner. An easy entry point may be one hour of watching presentations or launching an entry event. The goal of the first class interaction is to create a win.

The reaction you typically get when you give community partners an easy entry point is very positive. They have interacted with your learners, so they see the great things that you are doing. They know that you are going to value your relationship. Now that you built up some relational equity, you can begin to ask them for more of the same or you can up the ask. If you asked a community partner to watch presentations, you might ask them to take a field trip to their plant or their office. As you develop your relationship, you might ask them to come and do some workshops. Everything at this point depends on the link you and your classes build with community partners.

Here are some common errors that can stop a relationship from forming or hinder forward progress. Number one, people outside of the education world do not run their lives by bells and 4-minute increments.

Fail Story

I was working with Mrs. T, and she took the risk of inviting an outside adult into her classroom. We made sure the plan was solid, and her learners prepared well. The community partner was going to come in as a first timer to watch presentations and give professional feedback. When I went in to check on how things went, I was shocked to hear that Mrs. T was not happy at all with her experience. Here was our exchange:

Me: " So! How did it go? Did it revolutionize your classroom?!?"

Mrs. T: No! It was awful! He didn't show!"

Me: "He didn't show at all. Did he call at least?"

Mrs. T: "Well, he did show up eventually. But he was late. I ended up with 30 7th graders and no speaker."

Me: "When did you ask him to come in?"

Mrs. T: "3rd period at 9:24 am. He didn't show up until 9:30!"

Did you see the translation issue? In Mrs. T's world, 6 minutes of unscheduled time and 7th graders means more gray hair. For her community partner, 9:24 means that she probably wants him there by 9:30. Outside of the education world, 9:24 and 9:30 mean the same thing.

The second most common error when inviting a community partner into a classroom is to assume they have been in a school environment since they graduated. Community partners likely don't know your building layout and have never experienced a passing period as an adult. What do you think a community partner thinks when they see a passing period – chaos, fire, massive brawl, loose wild animals. To make a community partner feel at ease as they enter the building, it is a professional touch to have a tour guide meet them. A learner tour guide can begin building the positive relationship with a community partner before they even get to your classroom. A firm handshake, smile, and background information on your class and the project will begin to build relational equity. Your learners likely do not naturally know how to greet an outside guest. A couple of quick training sessions during lunch will help them develop the skills they need as a tour guide and to start building networking and presentation skills that learners need as they enter college and the workforce. A great way to test out your tour guides' skills is to have them practice with another teacher acting as if they are the guest.

The third error we often make when we invite community partners into our classroom is the "no follow-up" mistake. You and your learners have knocked it out of the park with a new community partner, and now you are ready for your next partnership. Don't forget to take time to thank your guest! A community partner is taking time out of her day to help invest in the future; they are making a philanthropic gesture. While they are not doing it for a thank you, it is nice to solidify their good citizen feeling with a thank-you letter. Not an email! When you visit the office of a community partner, you will never see a printed email thank you on the wall, but you will often see the handwritten thank you from a group of students. It doesn't always have to be a thank you letter, though. You may send an update on a project they were a part of or an especially exciting win you had with learners. Give the community partner as much of a win as you can.

Win Story

Susan is from a large school district that has a PBL track. As a facilitator who knows the advantages of community partners, she is always on the lookout for community partners. Susan has a wide web of community help when she is looking for authenticity to ramp up in her classroom. Susan was looking for first responders to help launch her next project. The standards and deliverables were all set up, but she still needed the perfect community partner to help launch. While making a quick stop to McDonalds, she found herself waiting in line behind a police officer. Knowing the benefit a community partner gives to learners, Susan jumped into a two-minute conversation in a fast food line and landed a community partner that was very willing to come. As it turns out the officer was actually in an outreach position, so it was her job to be present in classrooms. What a win-win scenario!

<u>Bottom Line: What story will your community partner tell others after they have been in your classroom?</u>

Where to Start

So how do you start connecting with community partners? Large institutions like children's museums and zoos typically have an education department that are seeking partners. When you contact education departments, they already have avenues created to assist your classroom. To solidify this partnership, you want to look for "win-win scenarios." How can what you are doing in your class also help them reach their larger goals? More established museums are one of the only places I recommend a cold call; primarily because the folks in the education department are waiting for you to call or actively seeking out educators.

Another place to start is with local small nonprofits. Executive directors want to tell people about their passion and their cause. The typical executive director of small nonprofits is available and their main job is advocacy. If you can help her solve a problem, they will gladly work with you. Nonprofit relationships can be a tremendous win-win scenario and is also a great avenue to teach your learners about giving back to the community.

Before you start spending way too much of your time cold calling every large business in your area, you probably have authentic audiences in your school district. Older learners love to present to younger learners and often you can find standards that align vertically. There are school board members, principals, superintendents that can come in, and this can be a great way to garner support for the great things you are doing in your classroom. Parents of learners are another good warm contact that is right in your district. A simple form going home may turn up some leads for community partners.

Once you see the benefit to your learning environment, you will begin to pick up community partners everywhere you go.

<u>Chapter 9</u>
Norms and Protocols

Norms and protocols give facilitators and learners a framework for learning. Without structure, you can't expect learners or facilitators to know the implied rules. The work of John Hattie shows that one of the top indicators that move the needle on learning is clarity. Clarity can come through the use of consistent norms and protocols. Facilitators and learners alike want to operate within a structure.

Norms are an agreed upon set of terms that help learning happen in a classroom. Norms should be more than rules though; Norms should be empowering and should be created through voice and choice. There is a big difference between, "Let's read over the rules of my classroom." And "Now we are going to establish norms that we will all abide by to help make this the best possible learning environment." An established set of norms allows students a voice in the process, but it should also allow them to have an ongoing voice. If a student has a problem with another student, the teacher may ask, "Which of our norms do you feel was not upheld?" Or a learner may come to the facilitator and say, "Mr. Steuer you are not following norm #3." In either case, it is essential for the facilitator to be open and professional when demonstrating and upholding norms. It is empowering to give learners a voice in establishing a classroom culture.

Protocols are another powerful culture building piece. Protocols are structures designed to increase collaboration, efficiency, and professionalism. Learners and facilitators appreciate the organization that comes with a protocol because everyone knows the rules and roles, and we all realize our voices will be heard. A protocol is used to protect the voice of the introvert and focus the voice of the extrovert. As we honor the rules of protocols, we will show learners that they don't have to be the loudest to be heard.

Fail Story

When running a protocol called Connections with my students for the first time, I used a timeframe I typically use for adults. This extended timeframe allowed for a full 3 minutes of silence at the end of each round. Excited about running a protocol and teaching my learners the value of silence, we all waited. While I very much believe in the importance of teaching learners the value of silence, three minutes of awkward looking at each other was a bit much! After reflecting on the protocol as a group, we decided we weren't ready to tackle the extended length of time yet. We changed the time frames and saw great success, and we eventually worked our way up to extended times.

Win Story

Using a modified tuning protocol, as adults, we often tune PBL project ideas. Each time we address likes, wonders, and next steps, a previously stuck facilitator will say, "Thank you! The group has helped solve my main obstacle. Now I have a lot of ideas to help me going forward." This experience happens over and over again. A quick 8-minute tuning protocol allows the expertise of the group to solve a problem. Tuning protocols serve as an excellent lesson for facilitators and learners: The smartest person in the room IS the room.

Bottom Line: Norms and protocols give everyone a voice and a safe, organized structure for learning.

Where to Start

How do you jump in with a practical set of norms
using protocols? The National School Reform Faculty
site has a fantastic list of protocols from which to
choose. I highly recommend their training as well to
help build a staff culture of professionalism that will
undoubtedly form your classroom cultures. An
affinity map is a high-value protocol to use when
establishing norms, so this could be an opportunity to
jump into both norms and protocols at the same time.
Please go to www.nsrfharmony.org to print off the
Affinity Map protocol. To help outline the process,
the facilitator will give the learners about 4-5 post-it
notes. On each post-it note, the learners will write
one norm/rule that is important to them. Once they
have one rule per post-it note, they will place the
post-it note on the board. As more post-its are put on
the board, student leaders will begin to organize the
post-its by category. As the categories are established,
the class will have a list of learner-generated norms!
Everyone's voice is heard from the quietest learner to
the most outspoken, and everyone's voice has the
same weight.

Chapter 10

Voice and Choice

Voice and choice empower students as they get to be a part of the process of school. Instead of school just being something that happens TO learners, we invite them to participate through voice and choice. School is a reality for learners, and when they get some choice in how they learn it empowers them. Passive or apathetic learners can become active learners if they are a part of the decision-making process. When you give any person choice, they have the opportunity to step up and participate.

Do voice and choice scare you? I think your answer should be 'Yes!' I meet with many teachers who are ready to give up all of their classroom decisions to the students, and I meet with teachers who will never give learners choice because the one time they did it did not go well. The truth is there is a continuum. On the left-hand side, you have a completely teacher dominated choice structure, and on the right-hand side you have anarchy! Neither is great, so you have to find your sweet spot. This sweet spot may depend on the maturity of the learners, or it may depend on your experience and learning curve with voice and choice, or it may depend on the project.

Implementing voice and choice is a growth mindset issue where you want to continually improve and make your way to the right side of the spectrum as appropriate for you and your students. If you hit anarchy, just pull back a bit!

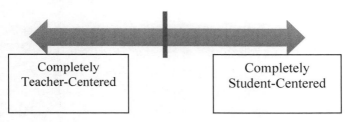

| Completely
Teacher-Centered | Completely
Student-Centered |

Voice and choice get lumped together when we talk about empowering students, which makes sense because they are similar, but let's define each separately and give some examples of how to get started.

Voice

Learner voice is allowing learners to be heard. Voice does not mean that learners always get what they want! A facilitator can collect learner voice formally through a learner voice group that meets once a month or weekly. These sessions can be to get feedback on how projects are going or how the culture is forming. While learner voice groups should not be an avenue for learners to get whatever they want, we should show some early wins to let learners know we are listening. As an example, a learner voice group may determine that there should be a new vending machine, more bathroom breaks, time to listen to music, and more structured work time. A facilitator may point out in the next week when she gives an additional bathroom break that this extra time is from the learner voice group. At the same time, she may talk with the voice group about the cost and school rules about bringing in a new vending machine. The learner voice group is a conversation, so it may also be a time for the facilitator to bring up some concerns she has about the way some things are progressing in the classroom to get feedback. Voice is allowing learners to be heard in an environment that has typically asked them to sit down, be quiet, and comply.

Choice

Giving learners choice is giving learners some control over their learning. Again, historically their education has been about control and compliance, so when we give them even the smallest amount of choice, they respond enthusiastically. Obviously, we are not giving learners a choice in which standards they want to engage, but instead which pathways they want to choose to meet these standards. There are still non-negotiables, but we need to define the aspects of education that are negotiable and give these choices to learners as often as we can. Choice starts to build some autonomy, which we know begins to create engagement.

Fail Story

Seeing how choice empowers learners, we set up a system of workshop rotations learners could choose from.

Me: "Sara, did you go to my complex sentence workshop?"

Sara: "No."

Me: "Why not?"

Sara: "You told us to choose our schedules. I didn't pick that one."

Me: "But don't you need help with complex sentences?"

Sara: "I guess, but it didn't sound cooler than the tech workshop or the team building

workshop. Maybe you should have a more
engaging title like you are always telling us."

And through the seemingly sound logic of an 8th
grader, mandatory workshops were born! Choice is
great, but sometimes kids don't pick what is best for
them. Data-based Need to Knows help give a
systematic way of assigning mandatory workshops,
but there is also the message here that while we want
to move down the spectrum of voice and choice, we
do still hold the right to assign workshops or
assignments.

Win Story

Have you ever had the 1pm lunch spot? We all know
every educational initiative is really run by the bus and
lunch schedules. If you get the first lunch spot, you
may be eating a brunch, but the last slot feels like a
forced fast. The Learner Voice Team brought up the
obvious idea that this is not awesome. Without a
Learner Voice Team, learners are just complaining
daily, but with an LVT, we can give a compassionate
ear and look for possible learner created solutions.

While discussing the last lunch period debacle,
the challenge put back to the LVT was to come up
with a solution instead of just complaining. The final
proposed solution was a vending machine, but the
current vending machine allowed learners to get
candy, which was not really a solution to hunger or
nutrition. After some lively discussion, the LVT came

up with a solution of selling more nutritious snacks at a set time between one passing period with the proceeds going to fund team activities. With some additional work but reasonable parameters, the facilitators agreed to allow nutritious snacks and the LVT had a big win. From that point on, facilitators could point to, 'Do you remember when we listened and put in the snack passing period?' Learners saw facilitators open communication which builds a trust that empowers.

Learner Voice Teams are a win. Even if they are not perfect to start, giving learners an outlet to speak their minds is always a good idea for building a culture of invested learners. You likely wish you had a place where you could voice your ideas and concerns, and your learners are no different.

To get started with an LVT of your own, you likely need to jump in and learn from experience but here are a few suggestions:

- Make the LVT a diverse subset of your learners
- Make it public
- Rotate learners on and off the LVT
- Ask their opinions…take some of them
- Meet regularly
- Tell learners not currently on the LVT to talk with someone on the LVT if they have an idea or concern

Bottom Line: Voice and choice will empower learners to be active participants in their learning.

Where to Start

Remember voice and choice is a continuum, so where you start is up to you and your students. To increase the voice in your classroom, you may add a couple of reflective questions at the end of your unit, "What did you like about this unit? What would you change for next year's class?" As you see the power of learner voice, you may want to have a group come in during lunch to talk with you. Adding choice to your classroom can start small as well. You may start with a choice of how the desks are arranged, which medium they would like to use to prove mastery of the standards, or simply ask them what they need to learn. As you begin to build voice and choice into your classroom culture, you will see students begin to advocate for their learning. Once learners know you will listen to them, they will tell you the best way they learn or if they need a workshop again. Once you start on this journey of voice and choice, you will have some hiccups, but you won't go back.

Chapter 11
Grading

What does the grade of a 'C' mean in your class? Does it mean a learner mastered the content but didn't do the homework? Does it mean a learner turns in assignments late? Does it say a learner knows very little about the content but is compliant and turns things in? If you have never looked at your grading closely, it likely means many of these things. When we jump into PBL, we are also going to be assessing Workforce Development Skills. Adding non-standard based content to our grades is gaining acceptance along with the idea standards-based grading, but we still want to make sure we know what our grades mean. The letter grade we give is one communication tool we have, but it has been given a lot of emphasis, so we should make sure we know what we are communicating. This chapter should help provide some practical tips and push your thinking to figure out how to grade what is most important for our learners.

We need to grade things we think are important. To communicate openly with your grades, it helps to break out your grade into buckets.

Separating out your grades is an excellent method which will help you communicate clearly with your grades. Even though we are going to be pushing you to infuse 21st Century learning into your classrooms and gradebook, we realize you are hired to teach a content area. To this end, a large bucket of your grade should be your content area. When you give a test directly related to your standards those points should go into your content bucket. However, if you are going to communicate clearly about your grade, you cannot decrease a grade in the content bucket if a learner turns in an assignment late. Before you close the book thinking anarchy is going to set in, you can still give or take away points for turning in late work, but let's create another bucket. A learner may have mastered the topics of genetics, but they are not well organized, so they turn in all of their work in a week late. If we don't have buckets, they might get a C in your class. Should a learner who has mastered your content receive a C? Maybe, but let's look at the communication through grades. What if you separated grades into buckets?

Group work has historically been disdained by students, parents, and even teachers. One learner does all of the work, and everyone gets the same grade, or one group members lets people down, and everyone's grade suffers. How can we effectively teach our learners collaboration and make sure their grade is earned by them? If we utilize the bucket theory, we can separate out content grades, self-discipline, collaboration, and presentation grades; we have a distinct advantage over past group work. We can create standards-based assessments that will individually show a learner's mastery. If we allow this individual content grade to be 85% of a learner grade, it ensures the majority of their grade is earned by them and in your content area. The other 15% can be made up of 5% self-discipline/work ethic, 5% presentation, and 5% collaboration.

> 85% Content
> 5% Self discipline/work ethic
> 5% Presentation
> 5% Collaboration

This balance of buckets allows for group work to be assessed, so we can give feedback, but not so heavily that it will overpower the content grade. Essentially, with this proposed balance, a learner can actively be in a group and still receive a 95% of their grade on their own. This example is one explanation of how a grade can be communicated. As educators, we need to be able to explain our grade breakdown to our parents and learners. Can you effectively explain why a student has a particular grade?

Fail Story

You get to the end of the project and learners have done nothing. I created a great project that was authentic and engaging. We let the students work in groups so that they could produce even more. A couple of days before they would present, we had practice presentations. I asked the first group to present, and they were miserably underprepared. The same with groups 2, 3, and 4. I stopped everyone and used the rest of the day to meet with groups to get them to where they needed to be. My big mistake was I waited until the end of the project to assign a grade. The majority of their grade was going to be wrapped up in a 5-minute presentation. I realized we needed benchmark grades for learners to grow into their presentations and projects, and I needed to be able to see where learners are in their learning to be able to help them move forward. I would now advocate for many benchmarks before the presentation; the presentation is more of an authentic celebration of the learning instead of a frantic and futile race for us to assign grades.

Win Story

Because you graded 21st century skills, you see learners display them. We want our learners to present well but are teaching them the skills they need. In elementary schools practicing 21st century skills, you can tour and hear from a panel of learners who will masterfully answer your questions. In fact, after I am greeted by a nine year old articulate tour guide and blown away by the panel answers, I am asked a profound question that entrenches me more in to this work, "Which of those learners do you think has an Individualized Education Program (IEP)?" I realize it is nearly impossible to tell who are the kids who are good at the game of school and who may struggle. All of the kids shine with confidence and eagerness to share their learning.

Bottom Line: You get what you grade, and you can only grade what you teach; therefore, if you want learners who have workforce development skills like collaboration, problem-solving, creativity, and grit, you must explicitly teach and grade these skills.

Where to Start

Ask yourself what it means to get an A, C, or F in your class. Look at some examples. Do you have some learners with As who are compliant and kind who don't know your content? If a learner received a C or F from you, is it because they failed your tests or because they didn't turn in their assignments? What do you think your grade should represent? If a learner turned everything in and participated in discussions but failed all of your tests, what grade would they get? If a learner didn't turn in any work but aced all of your tests, what grade would they receive?

As a next step, ask a colleague to engage in these questions with you. Dig into and try to challenge some of your beliefs around grading. Much of this conversation is also already happening, so see what others are saying. Type in "why you shouldn't give zeroes as grades" to Google and see where this takes you. Don't be afraid of the discussion. It will only lead to more intentional work for your learners.

Chapter 12
Conclusion

Hopefully, this book doesn't get stuck in the self-help section because it will take collaborative help to be successful. You can start out as the lone nut (google 'shirtless dancing guy), but you will need followers and collaborators to help you problem solve and innovate. The real key to bringing PBL to your learners is for you to live the lifestyle yourself. You will need to think critically about things you have always done, revise your work, make your work public, and do all of the things you are asking your learners to do. You must be a learner too.

Ultimately, the goal is not for you to be a great teacher, but for your students to become exceptional learners. Your job is to facilitate the awesome. I will not tell you it is easy; I will simply tell you it is worth it. You didn't say yes to this calling to help kids get to average. You committed your life to education to bring opportunities to kids, to show them they are an asset and a gift to the world, and to let every learner know they must share their talents with the world. To show them this they must practice these things in your classroom. They will not talk to professionals in the real world if we don't give them their first opportunity and show them how. We must model the learning behaviors and high expectations we have of them. We must have unending energy to bring more and more opportunities to kids who otherwise would not have them. Will they take full advantage of every opportunity? Of course not. They are practicing, but when we stick with them, they will find opportunities when it counts, and that is why you entered into this profession. Thank you for your continued dedication to the craft!

Fail Story

This book has taken two years too long to write. Possibly because I have been too busy doing the work, but more likely is the fact that I wrote it alone. If I had enlisted a partner or accountability group, I would probably have been done much earlier. Don't make the same mistake I made. You don't even have to commit to doing PBL yet, but tell someone you are thinking about PBL. Tell someone you are thinking about doing something different. Now you know the journey will have wins and fails, but did you pick up the main point? The main point of the book is don't wait to be perfect to get started. Start now! Start now, but don't start alone. Know that the wins build on each other, and the wins far outweigh the fails. The fails are small stepping stones to more significant wins.

Win Story

This book is a compilation of awesome, and would not be possible without incredibly awesome facilitators working on the front lines doing amazing things for learners. Share the wins you have on the journey, and don't keep the fails to yourself either. Share it all and move forward. Use whatever the current platform is to share with the world the greatness inside your classroom. We can no longer afford for your awesome to be behind closed doors. Share it and spread it!

<ins>Bottom Line: PBL can change lives. This includes yours!</ins>

Where to Start

[Learn, Jump in, Collaborate, Reflect] Repeat x ∞

PBL Stories and Structures: Fails, Wins, and Where to Start

Appendix

Passionate topics that didn't fit the rest of the book

7 Steps to starting PBL

If you have been thinking about exploring Project Based Learning but are unsure of where to start, here are seven steps you can take in your current classroom before jumping in.

1. Develop a growth mindset

Carolyn Dweck has cornered the market on this idea of growth mindset connected to lifelong learning. Start with her TedTalk and several good follow-up articles defining and redefining the concept of growth mindset. The general idea is we can all be good at math or piano if we have the right mindset. We just might not be there yet. A growth mindset is an essential first step in the PBL journey for both teacher and students because PBL is a process that you and your students grow into. We are creating problem solvers, not just good test takers.

2. Know your Standards

In Project Based Learning, we are looking to make connections to real-world problems. As you walk through the real world every day, it helps to know how your standards are grouped so that you can make connections. A middle school teacher in Lexington, KY, linked his US History class while watching Good Morning America. Because he knows his standards well, he connected the current event to his class, and by the end of the project, his students were in front of the Lexington, KY city council proposing a new city flag. By the way, Lexington did adopt a new flag due to his students' presentations.

3. Voice and Choice

Project Based Learning isn't about handing the helm over to students and letting the ship run into the rocks, but we are all about empowering students by asking for feedback and giving them choices to make. A smooth entry point here is to ask students how your last unit went. Ask them to provide you with "likes" and "wonders." When they have a wonder, act on it in your next unit. When students see that you are listening they will be empowered to be involved and engaged. As a side benefit, you will get feedback to improve your practice.

4. Invite a CP

Authenticity turns apathy into aspiration! A project with community partners can bring students to life. Bringing in an outside expert adds a sense of reality to a project that we as educators can't replicate. You get to see your learners 180+ days a year, which is great for building relationships, but a community partner adds a unique measure of engagement and authenticity to a project. A community partner is likely closer than you think. We had one facilitator who was looking for a law enforcement partner and found her in line at McDonalds! People are happy to help out with their time, and it can revolutionize your classroom environment.

5. Differentiated Workshops

Workshops might be a stretch if you haven't adopted PBL, but it is a such a valuable practice to personalize learning. In PBL, it helps to have the larger overarching project for students to work on while you are holding small workshops. Otherwise, differentiation can be tricky because what else are your students doing while you are holding smaller workshops? If 40% of you students bomb their quiz, what do you do? Review with everyone? Move on and hope they catch up? One of the strengths of PBL is the ability to differentiate and personalize the learning. For example, while the 40% of students who bombed your compound sentence quiz are reviewing with you, the other 60% have the long-term goal of completing their project to keep them engaged. If you haven't converted over to PBL yet, have someone co-teach with you so that you can hold a workshop. You'll love the way you can personalize the learning.

6. Professional Development

Project Based Learning is not a natural way of learning for us. Since the Industrial Revolution, we have been teaching in rows, so changing your practice isn't easy. Read a bunch of blogs, visit a PBL school, and then sign up for training. Find trainings that will mirror the PBL process so that you can feel the different flow of learning.

7. Jump in

After you try some of these in your current classroom and get some training, you need to make the leap. PBL get teachers back in their sweet spot. You got into education because you want to show kids all of the possibilities in the world. Nobody gets into teaching because you wanted to move test scores. Jump into PBL because you believe teaching makes a difference in the lives of your students. It's not the most comfortable road to relearn school, but I can tell you it is worth it!

Business and Education
Project Based Learning Can Translate

Driving Question: How do we connect involved partners and innovative educators?

When I was an Industrial Engineer, I was concerned about cost per package, missorts, and efficiently moving 400,000 or so packages through our facility during the night sort. When I jumped careers to be an 8th grade English teacher in a school with 70% free and reduced lunch, my new objectives were standardized test scores, discipline numbers, and student engagement. The former numbers were much more concrete, and I floundered for a bit at first telling students of the real-world applications I faced in engineering while handing out assignments that required them to regurgitate information on worksheets. When I found Project

Based Learning (PBL), my world began to make sense!

Before we dive into PBL, let's define the problem more precisely. Having been in both worlds, I can see the dilemma. Business partners are looking at the graduates they are interviewing and looking for a way to help these under-equipped hopefuls. Teachers have so much on their plate trying to reach moving targets that adding employability skills to their plate doesn't seem to fit. Both parties see the importance of equipping learners with 21st Century Skills, but both have trouble in seeing how they can help. Project Based Learning can translate into business and education to create natural opportunities for both sides to work together to attain their goals.

Project Based Learning uses some of the same engineering processes in the classroom that I had used in our plant: identify a problem, research possible solutions, work in a group to implement a solution, reflect and repeat. In the classroom, I found myself teaching students things that I knew were important to their future success and many of these could not be addressed adequately with a worksheet. I knew that a handshake workshop for a student in generational poverty could be a game changer, and it fits the workshop model of PBL. PBL allows us to engage the standards and address employability skills such as the four Cs - creativity, communication, collaboration, and critical thinking. Bringing in business partners to launch a project and share their expertise gives bank CEOs, plant managers, and lawyers a way in and my students a personal relationship with a professional. PBL is an equity tool to equip my students, who are in generational poverty, with the much-needed skills, confidence, and relationships they are not learning in other places.

An example may help show the process, so let's look at a project on genetic diseases enhanced by a business partner who is a DNA specialist. On the teacher side, the project is designed to address the 8th grade standards of genetics and informational text reading and writing. The final product for the students is to create an informational text about a genetic disease for a family who has just found out their child has a specific genetic disease. On the business partner side, the hemophilia society, a doctor who processes DNA for the State Police, and Jeanne White-Ginder (Ryan White's mom) will come in to add to the real-world aspects of the project. The gentleman from the hemophilia society launches the problem of families not having the right resources when they first find out their child has a genetic disease. Our expert from the DNA lab came in to present the basics (and some very advanced ideas!) on DNA that are a part of the standards. To cap off the project, Ryan White's mom came in with an inspirational keynote relating the student work to how it could affect real families. All three partners appreciated the invite into the classroom. All three added to the engagement level and content standards work. By the end of the four-week project, students were engaged, teachers addressed multiple major standards, partners affected the classroom, and 21st Century Skills were taught and practiced throughout.

How can you start this process where you are? It all begins with a conversation. One method showing success is having an education roundtable made up of school leaders, teachers, and business partners. The roundtable is a monthly meeting to discuss where the needs and opportunities are from both the business partners and the educators. A very telling moment came when the educators asked some questions to the business partners to help break the ice. When a business partner was asked what he needed from our graduates, he replied, "If they can communicate, work in groups, and think critically, I will get them their GED and teach them AutoCAD." What an eye-opener! The 4 Cs were the first things on every business partners list, and many teachers didn't see this as their responsibility. Outside of effective writing and speaking skills, business partners did not mention any content standards as their most significant need from graduates. Educators were also blown away by the availability of the business partners. Business partners have offered to launch a project, come in once a week, and even sit down with a teacher to help plan a project. If your business partner is a part of the planning process, you can be assured they are bought into the success of that project!

The answer to helping students attain mastery of the 4 Cs is not as far away as business partners or educators think. In fact, the answer may be one conversation away. Business partners are eagerly looking for ways to help in the classroom, and teachers want to provide the opportunities to their students. PBL can be a translating factor because the processes are already in place, but don't be afraid to start with a conversation.

ABOUT THE AUTHOR

Ryan Steuer passionately empowers those around him to see the great possibilities around them. Ryan does this by working with students, educators, nonprofits, and anyone who will stop long enough to answer a few questions. Project Based Learning changed Ryan's life to the degree that he cannot help but share it with others. Ryan also empowers his family of 5 kids, a beautiful wife, and 15 chickens. Ryan hopes his next book is about chainsaw carving.

Made in the USA
Middletown, DE
13 May 2019